Before Today

Beyond Tomorrow

Poems from the Multiverse

Doc Janning

Doc Janning

Cover Design by Elric R.A. DeVault

Copyright © 2023
Venetian Spider Press™ & Doc Janning
All rights reserved.
ISBN-13: 979-8-9890481-0-6

Before Today – Beyond Tomorrow

This book is dedicated

to the Multiverse

to this life

all the lives I have lived

and the lives I have yet to live

in the infinity of moments

Doc Janning

Before Today – Beyond Tomorrow

In Re: Doc Janning:

    Some of us know our purpose in life from the time we are small children. Others spend a lifetime seeking, yet never finding, fulfilment. Then, there are those who attain their purpose later in life.
    Doc is an artist who followed convention and career earlier in his life, but those did not allow for a satisfying degree of fulfilment. His art, writing, was an avocation which provided a degree of satisfaction, but did not, in reality, help him find his voice.
    His later years, and a near-death experience, brought a conscious decision to focus on what he truly loves, expressing himself in the voice and song of poetry. This time, however, rather than writing at his desk, mostly for himself, he made a concerted effort to become involved in the community of poetry, art, and music. He moved from solitude to active engagement, writing then reading his poetry in his resonant baritone voice, and sharing his thoughts with followers from around the globe.
    Doc has also created new opportunities for himself and his community to learn and partake of poetic language. He does this not just through writing verse, but by inviting others to celebrate and make it part of quotidian existence.

J. H. Mushkat Conomy, Ph.D. January 2020

To All My Family, Friends, Fellow Poets, and Readers:

The title of this book is taken from a line in a poem in the book, "Where Realities End." It is my firm belief that all of reality is the detritus of the past, which is Before Today, transformed on the forge of the now, into that which may become in the future, which is Beyond Tomorrow.

Below, less my comments in parentheses, is the first paragraph of a very long Wikipedia® article which spells out the current theories of a concept of which I became aware before the first theories came into existence. I feel the Multiverse is a conscious entity, which utilizes me, and, indeed, all creatives, as conduits, enabling its thoughts and creativity to come into existence. This is why the subtitle of this book is "Poems from the Multiverse."

Wikipedia®: The multiverse is a hypothetical group of multiple universes. Together, these universes comprise everything that exists: the entirety of space, time, matter, energy, information, and the physical laws and constants which describe them. The different universes within the multiverse are called "parallel universes", "other universes", "alternate universes", or "many worlds". (I also include the concept of microverses and macroverses as well as alternate timelines — though I consider time to be non-linear, and, essentially, a construct).

I hope you enjoy what I have tried to express in these few pieces from my body of work.

Doc Janning, July 2023

*Note: I love to sprinkle my work with unusual words. Enjoy!

Table of Contents

In Re: Doc Janning: 1
To All My Family, Friends, Fellow Poets, and Readers: 2
Unseen Moments 7
Resonance 8
Limitless Possibilities 9
Intimacy of Darshan 10
Echoes and Reflections 11
Ageless Moment 12
Glass-Winged Interludes 13
Traveling without limits 13
Merism of Time 14
Nexus 15
Limitless 16
Foreshadows 17
Transcendence 19
Chrysalis of Time 21
Forever Voyage 22
At the Edge of Existence 23
Infinity of a Moment 25
Reflections of Time 29
Terpsichore 31
The Edge of Reality 32
Samsāra 33
A Future of Unknowns 34

Palimpsest	35
Incantations of Forever	37
Mirror of Time	38
Unknowns of Forever	39
Time Within Time	40
Somewhere in Time	41
Sunshadow — Moonshadow — Earthshadow	42
Aeons of Dreams	42
Metaphor	43
Lyre of Light	44
Between the Real and the Surreal	44
Bal Surreal	45
Infinite Moments	46
Mytho-Poesis	47
Screed	49
Dreams and Memories	50
Cacophony	51
Premonition	51
Where Realities End	52
Wanderer	53
Late-Day Shadows	55
Cloak of Night	56
Cwtch	57
Quest	58
Sacred Journey	59

Before Today – Beyond Tomorrow

Fields 60

Nexes 61

The Door of Self 63

Gardens of the Sun 64

Becoming 65

I Am Me 67

Known — Unknown — Unknowable 69

In Moments Between 70

Mystic Voyage 72

Tangled Entropy - Bolide Heart In palpable presence 73

In the Terror and Ecstasy of Being 74

The Stillness of Being 75

Earthsong — Summerlude 76

OPERA 79

Poets 81

Cycle of the Future 82

Essence I 83

Essence II (ars poetica) 85

Ambedo 87

Moon-Shadows 88

Omen of Infinity 89

Chronicles 90

Mono No Aware 物の哀れ 91

The Only Constant 93

Oneirism 94

A Thousand Billion Stars	**95**
Embers	96
Silhouettes of Time	97
Calligraphy	98
Grace of A Fading Day	99
About the author:	*101*
Doc's Artist's Statement:	***102***

Unseen Moments

Walking
between worlds
in the bright silence of dawn

We pass
like ghosts
between night and day
in broad strokes of existence
and unseen infinite moments

And life
treads through time
a cryptic revenant of life

Doc Janning

Resonance

Gardens of sound
blossom and bloom
in the day after tomorrow
in symphony   song
and musical metaphor
of existence
to become
harmonies   oratorios   and canticles
of ariose ascension

They chant hymns   to the past
paeans   to the future
in legends and lore
of love   and life
amid silent sibilance
of kaleidoscopic colours
in eternal stillness
and dreams
of being

All flower
into worlds   of the Multiverse
intersecting   and converging
in melodies   and intonations
patterns   and inflections
to reverberate
through past   present   and future
a resonance
of infinity

Limitless Possibilities

In the cloud
    of limitless possibilities
        each an anaphora
            of the subtle,
            of the hidden
            of the unspoken
        where thoughts are spoken
            mind to mind
    we speed into
        our futures
            across all the worlds
                of everywhen
All possibilities
    improbabilities
        understood by accepting
            limitations imposed
            from within
            by the Self
        time as convoluted
            among cusps of being
                not inexorable
                and never not there

Intimacy of Darshan

Crossing stars
      on journeys of tao
      on journeys of karma
arcing
      above the galactic plane
      into worlds within worlds
flying
      thru transcendent aeons
      thru time within time
      in states of being and not
the rim whispers
      in arcane silences
      of eldritch darkness
      of places between
      in infinities of the Multiverse
      in dreams and embers of entropy
and existence is
      the intimacy of darshan
      the kundun of being
      the before of today
      the beyond of tomorrow
      the dharma of destiny
            and the Hineni of being

Echoes and Reflections

The Waltz of Time
dances through the Multiverse
in echoes and reflections

echoes
of galaxies and stars
reflections
of planets moons and comets

echoes
of life great and small
reflections
of existence

echoes
of being and becoming
reflections
of infinity

All weaving together
on the loom of forever

The dance is us
and we are the dance

Doc Janning

Ageless Moment

In the continuum of now

In the endless ocean of time

Reality
is but the shadow of a dream

An oasis of existence

longing

for itself

Lost

in an ageless moment

The moment

before

Glass-Winged Interludes

Traveling without limits
outside the time before today
and beyond tenebrous tomorrow
where ancient legends sing
what cannot by ears be heard
of effulgent light rays playing
in glass-winged interludes
among dancing sunset hills

Find remnants of the past
forgotten endless highways
and residues of other nows
'midst synergy and syzygy of stars
creating of their scattered dust
on the warp and weft of eternity
the unknown contained in a world
a foundation for the future.

Merism of Time

Before today
beyond tomorrow

lie other worlds

Worlds of memories

worlds of existence

worlds of dreams

All woven into the perception of now

the experience of moments

and the realities of time

Time which is indifferent

time which is uncaring

time expressed as change

Beginnings and endings

the merism of time

Nexus

In the space between
> between
>> before today
>>> and beyond tomorrow
>
> there is a moment
>> a moment
>>> of now
>
> a now
>> of limitless possibilities
>
> where lies a node
>> a nexus
>> amid distant drums of time
>> in a vortex of intricate language
>>> the colours of music
>>> and a kaleidoscope
>>>> of thought

It holds an anthology
> an anthology of life
>> life in armour
>> life in silk
>> life in all the intricacies
>>> impossibilities
>>> and improbabilities
>>> of the far side of never

Life which seeks
> that which seeks life
>> in the voices of distant longing
>> and the caress of infinity

Doc Janning

Limitless

The swell of dreams
shapes and contours infinities
of endless space and time
from canticles of stars
vantablack of dark matter
and songs of the Multiverse

Arcane legends of being
stream in echoing silence
among strings of galaxies
reflecting and refracting
in light shadow and colour
through limitless dimensions

And become …

Foreshadows

Between worlds
worlds of dream
and those of waking

amid hidden chthonian depths
of eldritch dimensions
lie arcane foreshadows

of before today
beyond tomorrow
and infinities of today

in empires of imagination
realms of fantasy
and kingdoms of surreal

Mystic ancient forms
emerge
from echoes of time

a concatenation
of dream and nightmare
in eddies of forever

silhouettes of the known
outlined
by the unknown

Doc Janning

refracting
through crystal stars
a spectrum of being

Canticles of existence
sung
on the far side of never

Transcendence

Time floods
into
around
through
and among
dimensions
within dimensions

It creates
destroys
galaxies
stars
and worlds

in the infinity
and transcendence
of being
of not being

It exists
in the tao
of the Multiverse
amid hidden reflections
of forever

and echoes
of all the colours
which ever were
are
or will be

Doc Janning

It is a timeless kundun
and darshan
of itself
an eternal refraction
and pavane
of Hineni

Chrysalis of Time

Chrysalis of time opens
revealing
past present and future

Kaleidoscopic wings of
before today and
beyond tomorrow

Pathways of the past
converge
becoming today

Trails to the future
diverge
into infinite futures

Its starry children
whisper
silent songs of forever

And fractaled life
revels
in love of itself

Its sacred fires
echoing
through the Multiverse

A journey of unknowns
resonating
to become

Limitless possibilities

Forever Voyage

Silent sacred skies
    of Island Earth
    steeped in eldritch blue
        of ages
    welcome
        traverse
            of troubadour Sun
            and dance
                of winds and clouds

All dream
    together
    on forever voyage
        through aeons
            and ages
        of the Multiverse
        across infinities
            of time
                and space
        into unknowns
            of an ancient future

At the Edge of Existence

    in the nexus
        of yesterday today and tomorrow
        of to be and not to be
    our past is
        but imperfect memory
        within the present
    our present is
        a concatenation of
            of hopes and dreams
            of happiness and fear
            of joys and sorrows
                imbruing into the future
    our future is filled
        with unknowns

Our past is future
    and future is past
        one never leaving the other behind
        in the crossroads of today

We are a creation
    of the sacred dance of life
        in all its infinite variation
    of those who came before
        in myriad generations
            and billions of years
    of our experiences
        in this and other lives

Doc Janning

Our thoughts distilled
    in the alembic of forever
We are not
    who we were
        moments ago
        days ago
        weeks months and years ago

We travel
    across the sharp horizon of forever
    through the mysteries of time
    and the frontiers of infinity
    seeking that which seeks us
        in the spaces between minds

We carry
    messages from the distant past
        to an unimaginable future
            and into arcane mysteries
                of unknown dimensions

We are
    becoming

Infinity of a Moment

Awakening
    in the heart of silence
    in the chrysalis of time
        and shadowed complexities of never
    in rewritten realities
        a mimesis and concatenation of life
    amid the unreal
        and psychic weavings
        in disparate mysteries and currents
            of imagination
            and translated aeons of dreams
    drowned in years
        and imbrued
            by ghosts of eternity
    wondering
        at possibilities
            and the time-worn chant
            of an unremembered future

Soar
    into luxurious light
        and sidereal nature of thought

Hear
    the plangent unheard
        across a shattered divide
            which cannot be crossed
    echoes of words
        words which have no meaning
            yet are understood
    an unintelligible rhythm of truth
        from ravelled tongues

See
> the unseen
>> through the prism of mind
>>> and its dithyrambic palettes
>>>> of colour
>>>>> in unfaded timeless
>>>>>> scenes

Taste
> a past
>> which is never the past
>>> with the tongue of the future

Feel
> the richness of sensual inundation
>> in the long hair of ages
>>> tumbling through aeons

Know
> of being and not being
> the meanings of numbers
> the inchoate pain of history

Ponder
> waves of existence
>> and enigmatic longing of the Multiverse
>>> which coalesce
>>>> on the other side
>>>>> of the stars

Dive
>	into unrelenting obsidian dark
>>		and chthonian depths
>>>			of trenchant eternity
>	into unknowing
>>		uncomprehending
>>>			grandeur and terror

Experience
>	non-time and non-space
>	pain and pleasure
>	fear and calm
>	hate and love
>	a conjugation
>>		of ignorance and knowledge
>>>			in shadows of illusion

Grasp
>	what we cannot grasp
>>		life love inspiration
>>>			and moments
>>>>				moments of untouchable
>>>>					indescribable
>>>>>						beauty

Journey
>	from nowhere to somewhere
>>		in the stolid trackless gulf of between
>>		on rivers and oceans of time
>	through labyrinths
>>		of conscious quiddity
>>>			and gates of nameless freedom
>	across worlds
>>		worlds unwritten
>>>			unknown
>>>>				forgotten

Doc Janning

                                        behind stranger
                                                worlds
        and the limitless within them
    to the place which knew
        what songs to sing

Flow
    through the Ley-lines of forever
    across the waters of life

Stravage
    tenebrous chasms and infinity
        of a moment

Subsume
    all
        in time-torn litany
            and throb of immensity

Learn
    to begin
        to become

Become one
                with infinity

Reflections of Time

Peering
    through clouds of dawn
        light
            paints sky
                in a coat of many colours
                in echoes
                    of the Multiverse

Mystic rise
    of Sun
        washes firmament
            in bountiful blues
                and reflections
                    of time

Elements of day
    assemble
        in vocalisations
            of life
                and ariose themes
                of forever

Patterns of existence
    emerge
        walking through fields
            fields of aeons

Sacred winds
    propel
        dappled dreams
            of yesterday today and tomorrow

Doc Janning

And day
      stravages
            amid swevens
                 of the future

Terpsichore

Infinite waltz of time and life
echoes
thru the Multiverse
a terpsichore
of arcane random

Elegant swirls of stars
strung   on esoteric mystery
stretch
across infinities
in endless   eldritch   dark

Universes rise and fall
appear
from cosmic nothingness
disappear   into entropy
a finite expression

A stage is set
amid boundless black
forever
as beginning and end
soar in a passion de deux

And the tao of all is

Be

The Edge of Reality

Outside
      uncertainties of life
           suspended in time

A half-seen
      pointillist image

The soft whisper
      of a kiss

Sudden passion
      and joy

Sunscape echoes
      flood memories
           unmingling mind and body
           to become beauty
           to sharpen the edge
                of reality

A distillation
      of feeling and
      of being fully present

And all dissolves
      into
           a moment

Samsāra

A year ends
    another begins

A continuing saga
    a continuing cycle

A time of before today

A time of beyond tomorrow

Everything changes

Everything remains

    and becomes

        In the infinity
        of the forever . beyond . forever

            Darshan
            of thought and imagination

            Darshan
            of thought and imagination

A Future of Unknowns

shadows catch fire
> in fading light
> and stretch
>> halfway to infinity
> seeing
>> in their blindness
>> what we cannot
>> the new worlds
>> the old
>> the cities
>>> which never were
> as time converges
>> diverges
>> and is
>> before
>>> it is not
> weaving a future
>> of unknowns
>> from the detritus
>>> of the past

Palimpsest

Peering
into
chthonian depths
echoing silence
and devouring dark
of time

into
its everywhere
and everywhen

into a surreal state of existence

and everything is

and is not

Light slides away in waves
through a labyrinth of forever
amid all the infinite nows
of yesterdays todays and tomorrows
and endless oceans of aeons

Eldritch colours and sounds
appear and disappear
echoing reflecting and refracting
across limitless horizons
exploring untold mirrored memories
in fragments of supernova soliloquies

Doc Janning

A kaleidoscope of torn-apart truth
an endless mitosis of dreams
in the densely-layered samsara of infinity
a vortex of intricate language
inscribed on a palimpsest of eternity
and suspended in a moment

And time is

                or is it …

Incantations of Forever

Light and shadow dance
through dendron crowns
amid warm dreams of day and night
in infinite chiaroscuro of time

An ekphrastic expression
of sunlight and moonbeams
in the kaleidoscope of Aeolus
'neath never-ending janus of sky

Life flourishes and grows
brushstrokes of evolution
in shimmering kiss of existence
from summer's golden horn

Incantations of forever
sing. a connected world

Doc Janning

Mirror of Time

The mirror of time
whispers
of past present and future
and the immensity of infinity
in crystalline languages of forever

It speaks
in hushed inscrutable tones
of naked memories and vesperal dreams
of the real the unreal and the surreal
and indigo times which never happened (or did they)

It reflects
eldritch beginnings and jussive endings
sacred merisms of existence
and myriad metaphors of itself
in untold yesterdays todays and tomorrows
of a Multiverse beyond space and time

It lets go
of what it is
becoming what it could be
and reveals
…
Everything

Unknowns of Forever

Painting a different set of stars
they pierce the canvas of infinity
in a revolution of normal

Galaxies pirouette
across stages of the Multiverse
on an undefined journey

Unknowns of forever
and the mutable prophecy of time
become
a mirage of being

And all is …

Or is it?

Time Within Time

Days pass within days
    and time within time

They display
    all the arcane beauty
        and terror
            of the Multiverse
                in echoes
                    echoes
                        of light
                        of shadow

Echoes
    meaning
        everything
    meaning
                    nothing

All converge as one
    in the tao of being
        and harmonics of ascension

To become ...

Somewhere in Time

Lyonesse and Avalon
Atlantis Rutas Shangri-La
Shambhala Cibola Cibalba and Ys
and others unremembered
unwritten undreamed

Lost lands and lost cities

Cities in the sky and valleys in the clouds

Lost in dreaming silhouettes and echoes
of times long past

Lost in mists of myth and legend

Shades and shadows
of a Dreamtime

Remembered
in story song and poem

Lost in millennia aeons and ages

Lost

somewhere

in time

Doc Janning

Sunshadow — Moonshadow — Earthshadow

Dappled shades of light and dark
refract
in ardent hues of life

And there breathe stars
in glowing galactic light
propelling
time

Infinity calls

Aeons of Dreams

Rivers of time
flow
through infinities
to explore
untold memories
in canyons of mind

And cafuné winds of forever
dance
in sensuous swevens
through aeons of dreams
to become …

Metaphor

In the embrace of infinity
the labyrinth of consciousness
and strangeness of adjoining worlds
poetry is become my shield
on the horizon between night and morning

The caress of time and space
explores untold memories
lost in canyons of mind
cryptic caves of ages
and hidden sacred abditories

Cafuné winds of forever
stir thoughts and swevens
amid omniscient tides of eternity
and dances thru aeons of dreams
searching …

The voice of distant longing
calls … from the other side of dawn
and all the infinite nows
of yesterdays todays and tomorrows
amid the endless matrix of existence

And I become metaphor
a metaphor of being
unexpressed in language
as I begin at the gates of the end
in thoughts which never were

Doc Janning

Lyre of Light

Sun arcs across the skies

Its lyre of light
warm to the heart

Igniting
stars within

And time
transcends

Between the Real and the Surreal

In a shadowed eldritch realm

between the real

a universe
lies

waiting

and the surreal

A kundun of tao

Bal Surreal

Time
    in ¾ time
    swirls spins and waltzes
        through itself

A grand ball
    un bal masque
    un bal surreal
    of infinity
    amid imaginings of forever

Stars
    shine brightly
        illuminating the scene
        illuminating the dance cards
            of galaxies and nebulas
      as each is born
          of aeons and ages

Each adding
    to the music and ambience
    in the everdance
        of eternity

All to end
    in the cadenza
        of entropy

Infinite Moments

Sailing
      on golden mangata
         'neath spangled baldaquin
            of ageless dark sky

Sailing across
      an endless sea of stars

Breeze singing shanties
      in the sails

Quiet susurration
      of water
         slipping past the hull

And there is only
      a before
         and an after

Infinite . moments

Mytho-Poesis

Wandering
    in moments
        of between
Each moment
    a now
    stretching
        into mists of infinity
            and shadows
                shadows of existence

Each moment weaves
    and breathes
        into the next
becoming
    a reality
        a universe
            unto
                itself

Each moment
    a summation
        a summation
            of past present and future

Each moment a journey
    a journey
        of dreams
    a journey
        of mystery
    a journey
        of life
    a journey
        within

Doc Janning

And I exist
      in the mytho-poesis
           of illusion
       somewhere
             somewhere between
              …

Screed

I dream of you
a dream
to find my way
in rodomel swevens
and on winding pathways
pathways of desire

I search
in the light-shadow
and tidal shifts
of a ruined heart
filled with feelings

I listen
to barely understood
mute alternatives
of veiled inner voice
'midst the fey scent of time
and eldritch rhythms of eternity

I dream, search, and listen
for echoes
for scintillas and traces
in the unremembered future
of what could be

Dreams and Memories

Distant dreams
        pondering life
                which begins and ends
                in endless moments
        and fragments of time

Distant memories
        of Earth, Moon, and stars
        of compounds and elements
        of heart, mind, and soul
        of … love

They sail on the seas of forever
        the sea of you
        the sea of Self
        bathed in mystery
                and riparian afterglow

They rewrite
        with vast crystalline light
        what they encounter
        in the serenity of thought
                and profound
                        contemplation

They rise
        in astral dawn
        across exquisite frontiers
        on the infinite edge
                of a boundless forever

Dreams and memories
        of hope

Cacophony

On indigo veil
cacophony of stars' tears
are touched by your soul
being breathed and unbreathed
on uncharted seas of love

Premonition

The scent of petrichor

exhales

A rich

velvet

sigh

A premonition

of poetry

and love

Doc Janning

Where Realities End

I am become everyone
I have ever been or will be
all the lives I have lived
and those I have yet to live
before today, beyond tomorrow

I have passed through gates
of a nameless freedom
as remote as the night sky
and the impatient stars
in a labyrinth of stellar strings

On the edge of beyond
where realities end
I see all and I see nothing
in a miasma of preternatural nature
as the future remembers the past

I seek, among wild eddies of time
and the primal rawness of ego
a path to unremembered truth
finite and vulnerable
in the kaleidoscope of life

I seek for my Self!

Wanderer

I am become
    a flaneur
I walk
    in the world
    in winds
        and moments
Moments
    of the mind

I walk through
    timeless forests
        landscapes
            and inscapes
                of wonder

I discover
    sensory
        and emotional
    horizons
        and mysteries
    mysteries of life

I become
    one
        with Earth
        with stars
        with the Multiverse
        with time
I am
    in an ageless continuum
        of change
All
    a surreal gift

Doc Janning

The gift

    of being

Late-Day Shadows

Colours

of simplicity

stack moments

among late-day shadows

in a song

which never

en....

Doc Janning

Cloak of Night

Night falls 'cross rim of world
douce velvet cloak spreading
becoming caverned baldaquin of stars
and silent indigo sea of Moon

Fantasy transforms to reality
and unknown waxes known
as infinite ALL intertwines
on ebon pathways of desire

Enter shadows of life
playing frolicking dancing
sky-clad and vulnerable
in exegesis of limning light

Silent eternal voices of forever
sing ardent soaring paeans
of patinated gleaming dreams
in wondrous ariose chorus

Perfection, imperfection
engulfed, swept aside
by consummate immersion
in ultimate joy of being

Cwtch

There is a fire in the storm
of me
A fire and a song
which seeks

It seeks for your fire
for the song
in your storm

That as one flame
we may burn brighter
to warm and calm our storms

To become more
more than hugs
more than cuddles

As our songs meld
in a chorus of cwtch

A place of safety
a place of peace
a place to grow
...
Together

Doc Janning

Quest

Winds of time whisper

among sand-grain stars

in unaware half-consciousness

remembering

they didn't know

they knew they knew

both unknown and

unknowable

ever questing for a past

of which to make

a future

Sacred Journey

On a sacred journey of spirit
a journey of realization and discovery
through an infinite ocean of stars
to a magick mystical garden
a garden of arcane secrets
where nothing is what it seems

Dreams tantalize to come true
as you discover your Self
in the unknown spaces between
the subtle, the hidden, the unspoken
of inchoate questions within questions
and immense primal mysteries

The effulgent nakedness of You
emerges, undimmed, untrammeled
from the misty scrim of within
in the throes of a silent scream
reverberating, echoing timelessly
as you are changed and reborn

Doc Janning

Fields

In the heart. of silence
    lie unburied sounds
        and questions

Questions
    embedded
        in fields of missing memories

They are memories
    memories of one place and another
        but not of either

They lie in fields of trauma
    personal and ancestral
        Interwoven
            with the inscape of a broken self

Fields of immense compassion
    and of compromise

Fields of resonant flow
    and the kaleidoscope of life

And the crystal bowl of time
    sings its song of healing
        in the intimacy of you

Nexes

I have lived many lives
within this one

       a child
       a student
       a fool

       a father
       a healer
       a leader

       a cook
       a listener
       an empath

and now a poet and a writer

I have lived thus in many worlds
worlds which have all overlapped

and intertwined in the polyglot

of time and the twisted road to me
as a poet and a writer

Just me myself and I
Just me myself and I
Just me myself and I
Just me myself and I

Doc Janning

A convoluted overlaid mix for which
a nexialist and interpreter I must be
speaking every entwined language
knowing where they meet each day

of time and the twisted road to me
as a poet and a writer

Knowing where they all may mingle
in this tornadic whirlwind life

of time and the twisted road to me
as a poet and a writer

Just me myself and I
Just me
              myself
                                      and   I

The Door of Self

Among ungoverned skies
    and forgotten stars
      'midst vantablack spaces
    on the edge of beyond

I am everything
    and I am nothing at all
    seen in shadows
        within shadows

I am a pointillist portrait
    assembled
    disassembled
    reassembled

I slip through realities
    and walk through the door of Self
        into the difference between
            myself and my Self
        into memories
           I should not have
              of an unremembered past
                  and the unknown future
                      of time folding into
                        itself
    into a cloud of limitless possibilities
        where all is coincidence
           of nothing I would ever know
        but …

                            I knew

Doc Janning

Gardens of the Sun

Amidst the gardens of the Sun
'neath the deep beauty of the sky
I find dancing prisms of colour
and sumptuous silhouettes
of immortal word-flowers

And take time

to be

Becoming

Phasing
between
among
across
and through
dimensions
of time
space
thought
and existence

Everything slows
into
a microcosm
of starts
and stops
yet constant
movement
ebb
and flow
rise
and fall

Neither here
nor there
not within
or without
nor somewhere
between

Anywhere
and anywhen
are long ago
and far away

or yet to be
and yet
so close at hand

Thought
is life
and life
thought
the unknown
amidst
the known

All mingles
melds
intertwines
melts
and blends
layers
upon
and within
layers
     Becoming

I Am Me

I am alone
         yet never alone
         for I am me
                 though I am many.

I am all my past mes
         and all the ghosts of pain
         and all the wounds
                 bloody and scarred.

I am life
         and many lives
         yet I am death
                 the destroyer of a world.

I am the flame of being
         and the burning cold
                 of not being.

I am everything
         yet the nothing which is.

I exist
         in the shadowed vastness
                 of everywhere
                           and nowhere
                 of everywhen
                           and nowhen
            as mapped
                 on the sliding scale
                       of infinity
         among runnels of time
         in the screaming silence
                 of this moment

Doc Janning

     of the next
     of the last
     of the infinite.

Known — Unknown — Unknowable

A poet writes the known
       the unknown
              and the unknowable

Sending ideas scattering
       on unmapped currents
              and tides of imagination
                      along the strands of time

To crest in supernal waves
       across the universe
              breaking ever
                      on the shores
                            of eternity

Imbuing thought
       of worlds forgotten
              worlds unwritten
                      worlds unborn

To grasp
       what we cannot
              of life and living
                      of love and passion
                            of inspiration

Ere we flicker
       into the obscurity
              of forever
                      'midst the echo
                            of words
                                  unspoken

In Moments Between

between
        life and death
                and life again

Healing and waking
        from within
            oceans of infinity
in synchronous syzygy
        of past
            present
                and future

Touching
        silken shadows of past

Letting go
        to 'compassing winds of time

Dancing
        in convergence
            of unknown forever
                we learn

Learning
        what life is
            as past fades
                across rim
                    of today
                into
                unremembered
                future

Learning
        life is love

and love is life

No hallelujahs
no hosannas

An Awakening

Doc Janning

Mystic Voyage

Pondering chanting elements
an epiphany in pools of stars
whispering a hymn of hope

Whispering a million dreams
into silver clouds of wind
and mountain lakes in the sky

Soundtrack of a mystic voyage
through a reprise of rapture
into a serene sea of floating flowers
outside of polychromatic time
and
anywhere and anywhen

IS

Tangled Entropy - Bolide Heart

In palpable presence
    of tangled endless entropy
        fractured luminous lexicon
            and fragmented future
seductive sitars sing
    of pinprick glowing gyres
        and gimbaled galaxies
in Bacchanal behind
    loquacious mirthful mists
        and random rainbows
            of dappled dark matter

Bolide heart bursts
    into constellations of love
        and jeweled paeans of passion
midst tremblant worlds
    woven of stardust dreams
        salient sensory questing
            and winding tunnels of time
to dance as a Dervish
    in ecstatic convergence
        of fragrant forever

In the Terror and Ecstasy of Being

Love is
    felt
        in its presence
                and its absence

Love is
    suspended memories

Memories
    written
        in cryptic calligraphy
            of time
                and of places between

Love is
    the surreality
        of a nameless world

A world
    woven in threads
        of past present and future

Love is
    joy and sorrow
        irretrievably linked
            in the inscape
                of time

Love is
    a plane
        a state
            a choice
                of existence

The Stillness of Being

The detached grandeur
              and stillness
                      of being
echoes
              in the candor
                  of stars
              with metronomic
                  merisms
                          in knowledge
                          of unknown past
                          of infinite future
              reverberating
                  through
                          caverns of time

Existence
              answers
                          in splendid silence
burgeoning life
              the ultimate
                        response
imponderable thought
              of possibilities
                      of unmapped pathways
                          pathways of desire

in the oneness
              of the Multiverse

Earthsong — Summerlude

Rushing waters
        cool sparkle of air
                soft rustle of leaves
                silken hillsides of green
                light-dappled wind-shadow
        neath slow dance
                of cloud-striated sky

Cantabile susurration
        of slow golden breeze

Ancient ageless arc of sun

Immeasurable dimensions of time
        each day scented
                with unique essence

Blue-gray stone speaks
        in numinous silent whisper
                and articulate sacred tone
                        of Earth and Nature
                        of ancient bourne
                        of eldritch magick
                        of birth
                              among the stars

Hint of distant music
        siren summons of seas
                and age-old calls of birds
        echo in plangent call of a jay
                elegance arriving
                        on wings of blue

Before Today – Beyond Tomorrow

All breathe from Gaia's heart
        midst sacred memories
                of hoar-rimed past
                        and unknown future

Within translated feelings
        and moments
                thoughts well
        of the impossible
                becoming
    half-conscious dulcet dreams
            of the possible
                coalescing into
                      phantasms

Memories of memories
        cross pathways of longing
            woven
                of sensuous sunlight
                of velvet shadow

Ethereal looms of time
        stretching, uncharted
            to the other side of the stars
            to vanish
                into the immense silence
                of infinity

I travel though my Self
        to find

    Me

And words
        words become
                worlds of light

Doc Janning

    as I become
           who

                  this place
                  this moment
                            says

                  I am

OPERA

Dark-clouded sea of sky
    lowering
        heavy
            pregnant

Giving birth
    to plump drops
        falling
            in thrumming
                strumming
                    age-old ballet
        swirling
            'cross rooftops
                of cities and towns
            thro' forest and field,
                o'er mountain and glen
        rippling
            'cross streams and lakes
                rivers and oceans
        washing air
            reviving Earth

Scents of rain and petrichor
        melding
        mingling
            in heady melodic bouquet
                roaring
                raucous paeans of thunder
                coruscating songs
                    of lightning
                and exuberant intonation
                    of cloud-limned Sun

Doc Janning

All weaving
        into ebullient, ariose
                rainbow chorus
                    of life

Poets

In limitless reverie
poets have always listened
to thoughts and songs
echoing through the Multiverse

Echoing from somewhere
somewhere between
between everywhere
and nowhere

They weave those thoughts
into fecund words
which ripen to phrases
and swell into lines

Thence to stanzas
and birth as poetry

A rebirth of distant memories
and what they have heard
from the shadowed vastness
of an infinite forever

And therein
lies the poet

Cycle of the Future

Dawn
      limns
           rainbow-draped river of sky
a light
      spun of nothingness
           within lidded eyes
                of stars
a light
      in a cloud
           a cloud
                of limitless possibilities

And melioristic wordless dances
      of the cavern of time
           folding into itself
    divide
           into before and after
                in the cycle of the future

Anaphoric words
      and phrases
           pose questions
                questions within questions
                    of the subtle
                        the hidden
                            the unspoken

All in another dimension

      The dimension
           of poetry

Essence I

Life walks
slowly   soundlessly
toward sunrise
shedding
vestiges of night

It treads
in measured pace
thru vibrant veils of dreams
across facile filaments
of dawn

And moves
in quiet moments
between
shores of dark and light
on arcane age-old pathways
pathways of time

It is expressed
in poetry
as a point
as a place
as a continent
as worlds within worlds

It is the restlessness
of a universe
seeking
itself
in dimensions
and unknowns

Doc Janning

It is a being
born of the Multiverse
to fly
through spangled velvet
of dark matter

Rivers of light
emerge
traversing
the infinity of forever
cascading
in echoes and reflections

Songs of vast silence
unheard by the unhearing
weave their fabric
through the essence of all
and Life
IS

Essence II (ars poetica)

At the apex of being
    lies a world
        a world of sound
            a world of words
                a world
                    of poetry

It is a world
    written
        in infinite warp and weft
            on the loom of existence

It is composed
    of stardust and comets
        experience and emotion
            time and life

It tells a story
    and sings a song
        in all the languages
            of the Multiverse

It is the voice
    of galaxies and stars
        planets and moons
            particles and waves

It is knowledge
    and wisdom
        transmitted
            and translated

Doc Janning

And is the essence
    the enlightenment
        the perfection
            of all

Ambedo

In velvet dark I look up and out
through the chasms of night
and beyond fields of stars

Through shadows i look into
the mouth of infinity
the mouth of time

I focus on the Multiverse
on the why behind the why
of its ever-changing map
the rhythms and chimaeras
of gravity time and illusion

In melancholic trance I look
at the wonders of entropy
the illusion of connection
and the arms of the ever-night

And I dream
...

of being

Doc Janning

Moon-Shadows

In hidden depths
        of misty moon-shadows
                words wait
they wait to be written
        by me
                by you
                        by us
in paeans of peace
        of hope
                of joy
                        and love
When our thoughts prompt
        they sail to us
                on bright mangata
Roadways
        made
                of moonlight

Omen of Infinity

Midnight
    black as loss
    streams silently
        on the sharp edge of forever

An omen
    of infinity
    amid shadows
        and ululations of time

Flows
    through prisms
    in light and colours
        of eldritch aeons

Unseen
    amid echoes
    among plangent stars
        and reflected Sun

Planning
    a future
    in unknowns
        and dreams of tomorrow

Pathways
    of desire
    through portals
        to become …

Chronicles

Shadows of night
soft ebon blanket of dark
sibilant stillness of silent stones
weave through dappled time

Chronicles of what has been
and dreams of what yet may be
are parsed in annals of stratified layers
stories told in palisades of aeons

Mountains robust with change
brittle to Earth's shifts and tectonics
rise and fall with drift and collision
amid life-pangs of Gaia's aeons

Mortmain of ageless epochs
and slow precession of axis
circle and cycle as the core desires
amid the visual vagaries of stars

Sol pulls its far-flung retinue
of which Earth is but one
in ageless spiral through dark matter space
destination a future inexorable   bleak

And with slow deliberate pace
all is moved in great gravitic spiral
through starred galactic arms
toward penury entropy and oblivion

Mono No Aware 物の哀れ
(Japanese - the poignancy of a passing moment)

The scent of light
    breathes
        within the ocean of time
    flows
        on infinite pathways

Mono no aware
    ripples
        across
            planes of forever

It exists
    yet
        does not
            in all the colours
                music and magick
                    of the Multiverse

From it
    transcendent breath
                a   new love
        rises
to become
    silent visions
        of peace
            home
                cwtch*
                  and one

Doc Janning

All growing
      in mystic dawn
           of dreams
                beginnings
                      unknowns
                            and a future
                                of ...

The Only Constant

Treading
      through aeons of
           days and nights
           dawns and dusks
     amid canyons of cloud

Aware and unaware of
      daylight and dark
      sunlight moonlight and starlight
         islands of sky gleam
             in sapphire and gold
                 silver and velvet

Wandering through
      dreaming seasons of
      time and life
         amid Aeolus' whispers and roars

Portals open
      thresholds are crossed
      into vistas of
         knowns and unknowns

Ephemeral becomes real
      in the breath and chimaera of
         colours passing through
         the kaleidoscope of ages

All processing
      majestically slowly
         but as quickly as
             a sprag of lightning

And the only constant is … change

Oneirism

Star-jeweled voices of time
    taste the zephyrs
        of unfinished love
      and
            whisper of a past
              which is never
                the past

Memories walk
    unbidden
        into the unknown
           the unknowable
              and seductive thought
              of what
                  might have
                      been

Souvenance smiles
    across the edge of infinity
        where words become worlds
           of magick
              spun of stardust
                  and dreams

A Thousand Billion Stars

Evening softly draws

Sun into dusk

(ghost of the day)

as secret voice

of infinite night

calls in eldritch tones

through warrens of time

and darkness rushes

on fey silent wings

infusing magick

into echoing caverns

of ageless black sky

melding and blending

with lambent shine of

a thousand billion stars.

Embers

Embers of dying stars
fly   through space and time
bearing remnants of what was
on journeys aeons   ages long

On pathways of dimensions
of universes   and space
become gleam and glow of new-born stars
in coloiurs never seen

Traceries of their light   echo and play
reflect refract twist and bend
across leas of unseen matter
across oceans and seas of ever

Becomes swirling entourage
planets and moons asteroids and comets
amid shifting shadows
of entropy

Silhouettes of Time
    e x p a n d
          without
                        l i m i …
limning the everywhere
    and everywhen
        of all
in transcendent dance
    of infinite wonders

Lingering arcane echoes
    of life
resound
    in scent and colour
    in spikenard and gold
sing
    in ariose ecstasy
        of forever
a sensual feast
    of silent joy
an endless Phoenix-cycle
    of scant and plenty

Seas of entropy await

Denouement
    of all
        which will be
        which has been

Cold steady-state
    of the end

Doc Janning

Calligraphy

Stars of memory
    spangle dark baldaquin
        of nighted supernal inscape
            in plaintive chiaroscuro

It is a janus
    a janus
        of past dreams
            saudade of present
                and a future
                    a future
                        which will
                            never
                              be

And I am become revenant
    a remnant
        of a netherworld
            a world
                which never was

And all ends
    or does it
        in lingering shadows
            infinite shadows
                in the maelström
                      the maelström
                          of existence

Written
    written in obscure calligraphy
        the calligraphy
            of time

Grace of A Fading Day

In the grace of a fading day
      the space between land and sea
      the space between light and dark
      the time between past and future

Within infinite moments
      in regions of wisdom and dreams
      on a quest of imaginings and symbols
      in unplumbed depths of astral history

The infinite inexplicable penultimate
      in the luminous sound of ecstasy
      in the sensation of a wing
      a wing gliding across strings of an instrument
          in the sonority of affirmation

And time. shrouded in shadow reveals
      the semblance of existence
      unknown words sung in arcane voices
          and daydreams of spiders
      everything. everywhere. everywhen
          and. infinity

Doc Janning

About the author:

Doc Janning, the 80-year-old Inaugural Poet Laureate of South Euclid, Ohio, is a poet, author, educator, longtime Scout Leader, and retired Podiatrist. He has created Ekphrastic Poetry for Heights Arts in Cleveland Heights, OH, and for Cleveland Photo Fest. He has been a Writer-in-the-Window at Appletree Books for National Novel Writers' Month. He has been a featured reader for many events, a visiting instructor in poetry for fourth graders at a school in Tennessee, and the moderator/instructor for a workshop on ekphrastic poetry in Florida.

Doc, in his capacity as Poet Laureate, reads for every meeting of the South Euclid City Council, for all major holidays, and at any civic event for which he is asked; sometimes with a company of local poets. He has also been "loaned" to the City of Lyndhurst for their Annual Independence Day Concert, and to the Cuyahoga County Council for their swearing-in ceremony and that of their new County Executive, Chris Ronayne.

When the National Federation of State Poetry Societies held its Annual Conference in joint session with that of the Ohio Poetry Association in June, 2022, Doc served on a panel discussing The Power of Literary Citizenship. And, In August 2023, he read as a selected Poet Laureate at the Ohio Poetry Association's Poetry Showcase at the Ohio State Fair.

Doc's work has been included in 30 anthologies, with three of his poems included in the most recent one," A Poem for Cleveland," issued in June 2023 by Red Giant Books.

Doc's favorite quote is by the late Rod McKuen: "It doesn't matter who you love or how you love, but that you love."

Doc's Artist's Statement:

"As Inaugural Poet Laureate of South Euclid, an Ekphrastic Poet for both Heights Arts, where I was Literary Artist of the Month for March 2020 and January 2023, Cleveland Photo Fest in 2019, and a Writer-in-the-Window for National Novel Writing Month in 2019, I proselytize for poetry in South Euclid and the wider community. I have visions of poetry workshops and readings in our schools, in every library, at senior centers, in rehab facilities, and juvenile detention centers.

I communicate with other poets locally, regionally, nationally, and around the world, working toward these goals.

We all have within us a spark of creativity, sparks which need to be fanned and fed if they are to become reality. Too many who have the impulse to write or have written are disparaged by others and never begin or never share what they have created. I want to engage, encourage, and enable poets and writers of every genre, young or old, new to the craft or well-seasoned.

My intent: To be among those who fan and feed those sparks, that they may become flames."

Milton Keynes UK
Ingram Content Group UK Ltd.
UKHW022258271123
433389UK00006B/324